Dedications

To the memory of a champion who attained his dreams while inspiring others — Dr. Angela O. Terry, niece

To my loves: Vernie, Addie, Maya — Kristy Nerstheimer

To my family, two girls Adira, Haley Rose and Doña Rosa "la bendición abulea" — Christian Paniagua

A portion of all sales will be contributed to First Base Enterprises, comprised of the heirs of John Jordan "Buck" O'Neil, Jr. and to the Negro Leagues Baseball Museum, as he was one of the original founders.

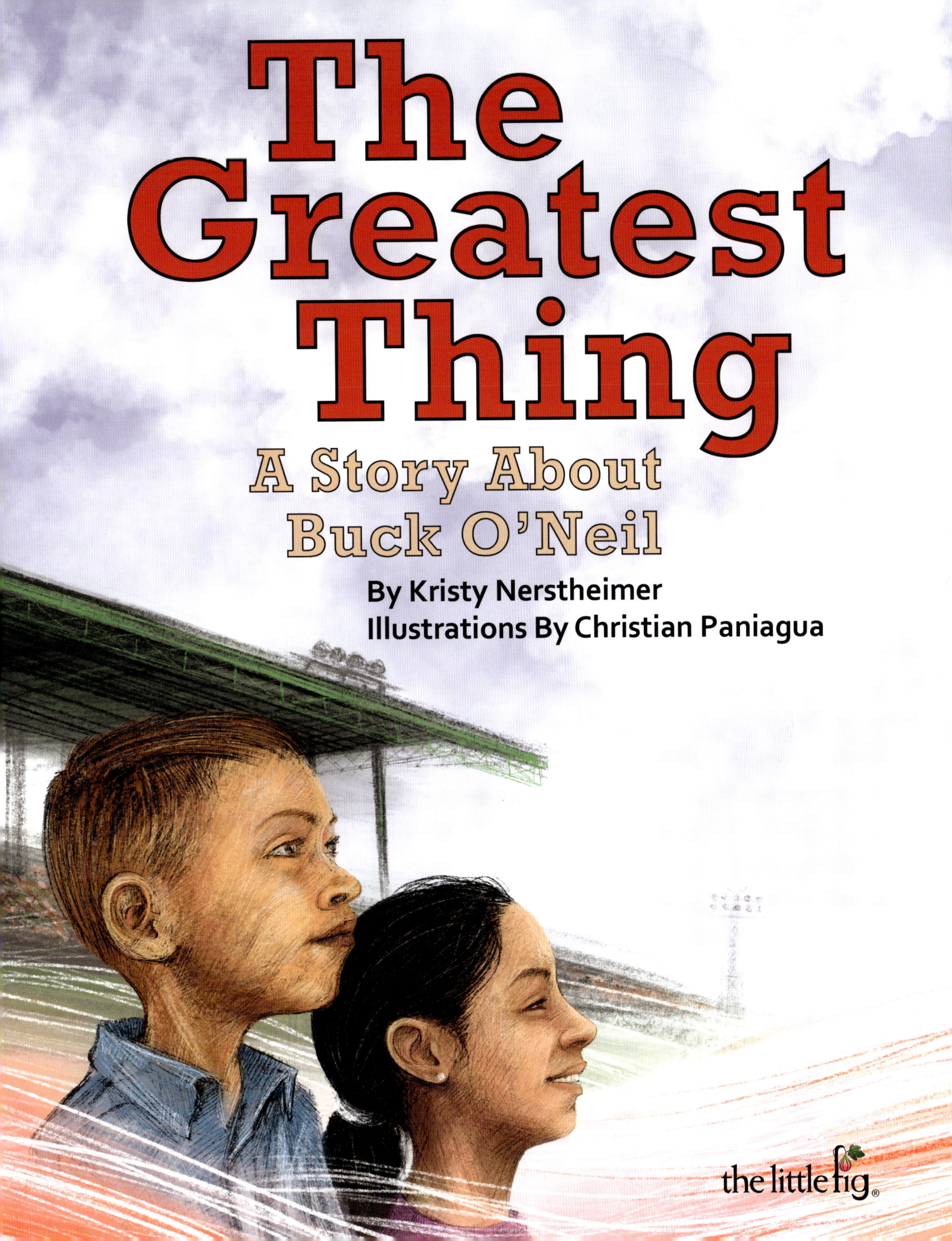

I am so lucky I got to play the greatest sport there ever was.

BASEBALL!

When I was a small boy, my mama made me a ball with socks tied around a rock. I played for hours and hours until it was too dark to see. That's just what you did when you were baseball crazy like me. My papa played too.

I loved going to watch him on the field. He even let me be the bat boy. I hammed it up with the older guys, and they liked having me around. When they threw the ball, I'd catch it with my big hands.

Baseball was an American pastime, and everyone enjoyed keeping up with the different teams. But back in those days, everything was segregated. Black and white people couldn't go to the same schools,

eat at the same restaurants, stay at the same hotels, or even play on the same teams. It was tough and unfair, but that's the way life was back then.

My papa subscribed to all the black newspapers so we could read about our favorite teams and players. I wore out the pages from reading them so much. Afterward, I'd run outside and pretend to be those players.

When I saw black players on those pages, I started to see the possibility of me becoming a baseball player too.

The most important thing I needed to do was practice, and I did whenever I could. I worked hard in school too. When I found out a high school was being built in my neighborhood, I hoped I could play baseball there. But my grandmother told me only white kids would be able to attend.

I cried and cried, but she calmed me down and told me someday things would change. When they did, I'd be ready. I kept working hard at my studies and even harder at baseball.

My principal, sweet Miss Booker, saw some potential in me. Where I lived, black kids could only go to school through the 8th grade. But Miss Booker taught us at night and during the summer so we could get a proper education. As luck would have it, I was able to get a scholarship

playing ball in a different town where black students could attend. It was hard to say goodbye to my family, but they knew I had to chase my baseball dream.

My dream finally came true when I started playing in the Negro Leagues. I earned a spot playing first base for the Kansas City Monarchs. Now that was a time! I played with Satchel Paige, the best pitcher ever.

James "Cool Papa" Bell was the fastest man I'd ever seen. We called him "Cool Papa" because he was so easygoing.

I didn't do too badly myself. I hit for the cycle: a single, a double, a triple, and a homerun all in one game. What a day! I also played in

three all-star games. We won four pennants and the Negro Leagues World Series. I will never forget those days on the team.

Black baseball was fast, not like white baseball. We'd steal bases, bunt, and slide into home. Folks loved to gather at the barber shop to talk about the exciting games. Of course, life was still hard because of segregation.

The Negro Leagues had some of the best athletes in the country, yet we weren't allowed in many hotels or restaurants. I was just happy playing, even when I had to eat stale sandwiches on the back of our team bus.

Finally, Branch Rickey, an owner of the Brooklyn Dodgers, took a chance and signed Jackie Robinson to play in the major leagues. This opened the door for all of us. We celebrated and celebrated! It was difficult for some people to accept, but Jackie was tough. He proved himself. It was an exciting time.

I never made it to the majors as a player, but I did become the first black coach in Major League Baseball with the Chicago Cubs. Later, I scouted for the Kansas City Royals. As more black players signed on to the majors, the Negro Leagues began to dissolve. I didn't want those players to be forgotten, no sir. They were a part of history. Yes, history.

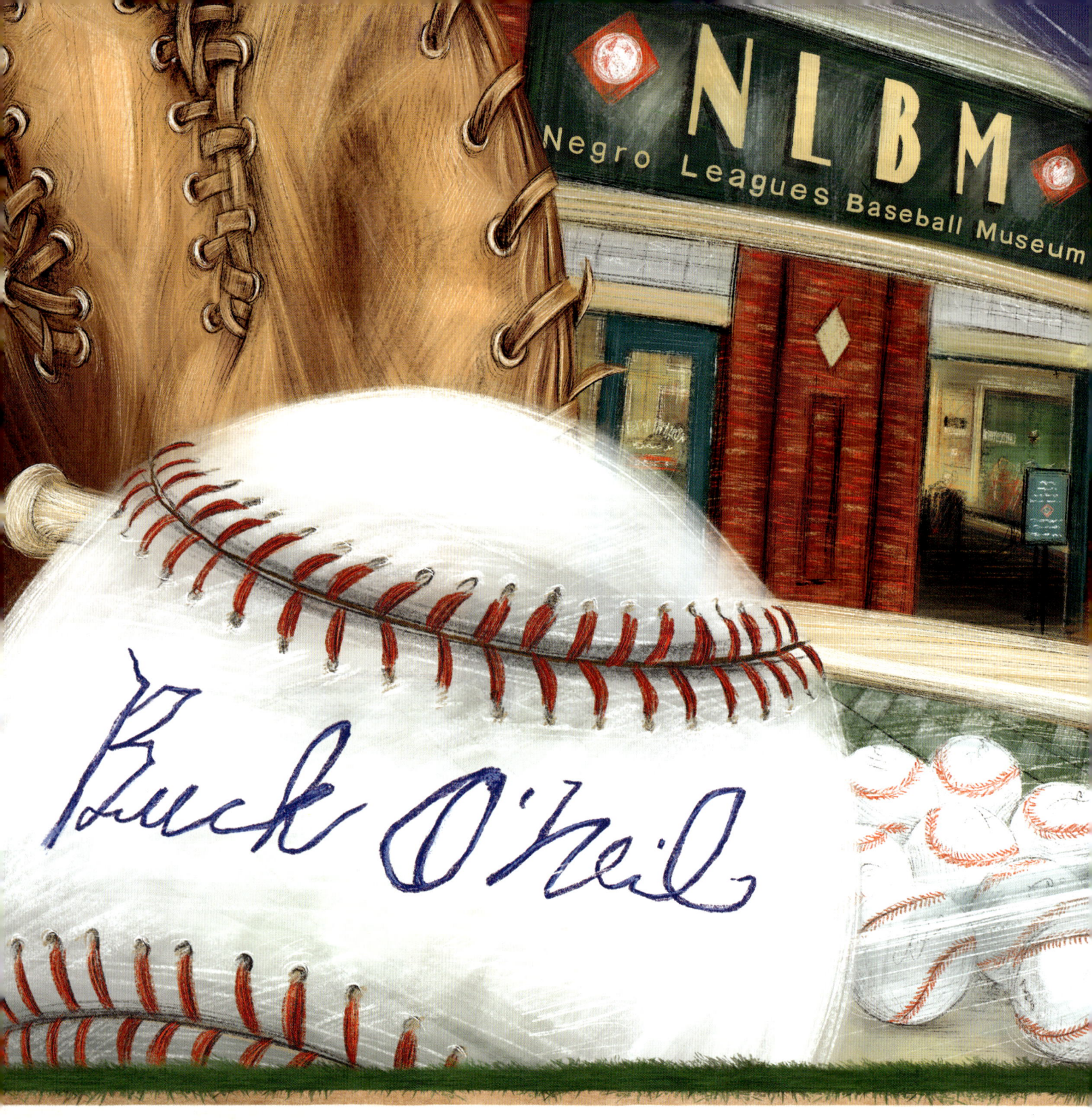

And here we are at the Negro Leagues Baseball Museum. There's no better place for you to be, right here, right now. I am honored to have been a ballplayer in the Negro Leagues because we helped change the world. We paved the way for Jackie Robinson and others.

We showed everyone it was time to move past the color of a person's skin. Some ask if I hated people for the way we were treated back then. But I never learned to hate. I can't hate another human being! In fact, I feel love. Agape, man. An overflowing love.

Step back in time to learn about an important part of baseball's history. Do me a favor now, come on, sing along…the greatest thing…in all my life…is loving you. The greatest thing. In all my life. Is LOV-ing YOU.

That's right, I will never stop loving baseball
and I will never stop loving YOU!
John Jordan "Buck" O'Neil Jr.

Author Notes

John Jordan "Buck" O'Neil was born in Carrabelle, Florida, on November 13, 1911. In 1920, his family moved to Sarasota, Florida, where his love for baseball grew and grew. Buck couldn't attend Sarasota High School because of segregation. Years later, the high school awarded Buck an honorary diploma, one of Buck's greatest joys. He loved looking out in the audience and seeing all the African American students. It meant inclusion was alive and well in Sarasota.

At the age of 12, Buck began playing on a semi-pro team called the Sarasota Tigers. At the age of 94, Buck was one of the oldest players to bat at the Northern League All Star game. For over 80 years, Buck devoted his life to baseball. As a young adult, he played on several barnstorming teams before landing a spot in the Negro Leagues, first with the Memphis Red Sox in 1937, and then as first baseman with the Kansas City Monarchs where he played from 1938-1942.

Buck missed playing with the famous Jackie Robinson because he left the league in 1943 to proudly serve his country during WWII. He returned to play with the Kansas City Monarchs when his tour of duty ended in 1946. Buck became their manager because of his leadership skills and the way he encouraged his teammates. He held the position from 1948-1955.

In 1955, the Chicago Cubs hired Buck as a scout for the team. He discovered talented players and connected with their families. He attended church and ate dinner in their homes which created a lasting bond. Buck then worked with the players during spring training. Other teams complained about his presence because he was black. The Cubs valued his skills so much, they decided to solve the problem and made him a coach in 1962. Buck O'Neil became the first African American coach in the major leagues. He worked with the Chicago Cubs for 33 years.

In 1988, Buck returned to his original baseball home in Kansas City. Until his death in 2006, he worked as a special assignment scout for the Royals. He sat behind home plate at every game, took notes, kept track of stats, and observed every play. His charismatic personality made him a crowd favorite. There wasn't a hand he wouldn't shake or a hug he wouldn't give.

Buck made it his mission to ensure the players from the Negro Leagues would not be forgotten. Not only was he one of the founders of the Negro Leagues Baseball Museum, he worked tirelessly to induct those players into the Baseball Hall of Fame in Cooperstown, New York. He often gave speeches about the museum and the outstanding players from the leagues. Crowds fell in love with his charming spirit and his immense positivity. He ended most speeches by having the crowd join hands to sing "the greatest thing in all my life is loving you."

In 2006, 17 players from the Negro Leagues were inducted into the Hall of Fame in Cooperstown. However, Buck did not receive enough votes to be inducted himself. Fans were angered by this injustice, but Buck's larger-than-life personality took it in stride. He was even one of the speakers at the induction ceremony. Buck died later that same year on October 6 at the age of 95.

Because of Buck's determination, dedication, and immense spirit, he became known as one of baseball's most beloved ambassadors. In a time of segregation and prejudice, Buck persevered. He always showed love and acceptance. Buck not only made the game of baseball better, he spread his joy to anyone who met him.

Posthumously, Buck was given the Presidential Medal of Freedom by President George W. Bush, the highest honor given to a civilian. The Baseball Hall of Fame dedicated a life-sized bronze statue of him and created the Buck O'Neil Lifetime Achievement Award. This award is given to those who make an extraordinary difference in baseball. And at every Kansas City Royals' game, an honored recipient sits in the Buck O'Neil Legacy Seat. The recipient is someone who exudes Buck's spirit and contributes significantly to the community. Buck O'Neil's impact on baseball and his zest for life make him a true legend.

Acknowledgements

A very special THANK YOU to these and so many others who helped bring Buck's story to life:

Bob Kendrick, President of the Negro Leagues Baseball Museum
Dr. Ray Doswell, Curator of the Negro Leagues Baseball Museum
Dr. Angela O. Terry, Buck O'Neil's niece and head of the
    First Base Enterprises
John Boyd Martin, Portrait Artist (Buck's original portrait currently
    hangs in the NLBM)
Dr. Robert Lee Hill, Minister Emeritus of Community Christian Church,
    Board Member NLBM
Thomas S. Busch, Attorney at Law
Katherine Steiner, MLB Legal Coordinator
Major League Baseball's (MLB) Chicago Cubs
Patrick Manaher, Authentics and Archives – Chicago Cubs
Kelly King, Chicago Cubs Manager, Graphics – Cubs Productions
    Wrigley Field
Park University's Nonfiction Writers Intensive (NWI)
Envisioned by Dr. Kathleen Howe, Director of Park University's
    Watson Literacy Center
Developed and instructed by the team at The Little Fig®
Jennifer C. Bailey, editor and NWI instructor
Tessa Elwood Sosa, NWI instructor
Adira and Haley Rose Paniagua
Judy Hyde, copy editor
Joe Posnanski

Online Sources

Buck O'Neil: https://www.chicagotribune.com/news/ct-xpm-2006-10-08-0610080305-story.html

Buck O'Neil: Beginning Career: https://www.youtube.com/watch?v=N3FE-xZxzeQ

Buck O'Neil Biography: https://www.notablebiographies.com/supp/Supplement-Mi-So/O-Neil-Buck.html

Buck O'Neil Chicago: https://www.youtube.com/watch?v=2Bd8PgMs3qo

Buck O'Neil Chicago Cubs: https://www.mlb.com/news/cubs-made-buck-o-neil-mlb-s-first-black-coach-c216445780

Buck O'Neil: First African Coach and Scout: https://www.kshb.com/lifestyle/tasteseekc/buck-oneil-first-african-american-mlb-coach-scout-left-major-impact-on-kansas-city

Buck O'Neil: Growing Up: https://www.youtube.com/watch?v=v3rtNgk9vcs

Buck O'Neil Hall of Fame: https://baseballhall.org/discover-more/awards/890

Buck O'Neil: Hall of Fame Induction Speech: https://www.youtube.com/watch?v=LtE2I6jsung&t=335s

Buck O'Neil: Negro League Museum: https://www.youtube.com/watch?v=wCnCuithBw4

Buck O'Neil: Segregated School System: https://www.youtube.com/watch?v=Qnc1RdEsncY

Buck O'Neil: Ty Cobb and Prejudice: https://www.youtube.com/watch?v=l7zYopq-dFs

Discovering Greatness: https://www.youtube.com/watch?v=tR-D-g79x_w&t=6s

Dr. Doswell and the Negro League Baseball Museum: https://www.youtube.com/watch?v=oFtSdjucCIA

Introducing Buck O'Neil: https://www.youtube.com/watch?v=ih-qSjU7ObU

Keith Olbermann Remembers Buck O'Neil: https://www.youtube.com/watch?v=o8wxoeyhQE4

Memories of the Negro League: https://www.youtube.com/watch?v=WgxrsamGiDw

Negro League Museum: http://www.nlbemuseum.com/history/players/oneil.html

Negro League Museum: https://www.youtube.com/watch?v=Cn7DvawDBwU

Remembering Buck O'Neil: https://sportsworld.nbcsports.com/buck-oneil-10-years-later/

Sources

Gall, Jeff and Gall, Micah Buck O'Neil: Baseball's Ambassador. Missouri: Truman State University Press. 2016

Nelson, Kadir. We Are the Ship: The Story of Negro League Baseball. New York: Hyperion, 2008.

O'Neil, Buck (with Steve Wulf and David Conrads). I Was Right On Time. New York: Simon and Shuster, 1996.

Posnanski, Joe. The Soul of Baseball. New York: Harper Collins, 1997.

Copyright

Text copyright © 2020 Kristy Nerstheimer
Illustrations copyright © 2020 Christian Paniagua
All rights reserved. No part of this book may be reproduced or transmitted in any form or by any means that are available now or in the future, without permission in writing from the copyright holder and the publisher.

Published in the United States of America by The Little Fig ®.
The logo for The Little Fig is a registered trademark.

Hardcover ISBN-13: 978-1-63333-053-5

Library of Congress Cataloging-in-Publication Data is availble

Printed in the United States of America

Visit or contact us at

the little fig.

P. O. Box 26073
Overland Park, KS 66213
www.thelittlefig.com